Canadian Brass

Wedding Essentials

CONTENTS

T0052910

This book is arranged for 2 B-flat trumpets, French horn, trombone, and tuba. The music in this book is from the personal library of Canadian Brass and has been performed and recorded by Canadian Brass.

Other books from Canadian Brass

Book of Beginning Quintets

Book of Easy Quintets

Book of Favorite Quintets (intermediate)

Book of Advanced Quintets

On Broadway

Rodgers and Hammerstein

Play Along with Canadian Brass (easy level)

Play Along with Canadian Brass (intermediate)

Canadian Brass Christmas Carols

Hymns for Brass

Immortal Folksongs

Favorite Classics

Visit *www.canadianbrass.com* for recordings from Canadian Brass

7777 W. BLUEMOUND RD. P.O. BOX 13819 MILWAUKEE, WI 53213

For all works contained herein:
Unauthorized copying, arranging, adapting, recording or public performance
is an infringement of copyright. Infringers are liable under the law.

Visit Hal Leonard online at
www.halleonard.com

"AIR"
from *Water Music*

Handel
(1685-1759)
Arranged by Walter Barnes

2003, 1983, Canadian Brass Publications LTD
International Copyright Secured

2

LARGO

from *Xerxes*

George Frideric Handel
(1685-1759)
arranged by Walter Barnes

2nd B♭ CORNET/TRUMPET

2003, 1988, Canadian Brass Publications LTD
International Copyright Secured

PRAYER

from *Hansel and Gretel*

2nd **TRUMPET**

Engelbert Humperdinck
(1854-1921)
arranged by Henry Charles Smith

2003, 1989, Canadian Brass Publications LTD
International Copyright Secured

AIR ON THE G STRING
from Suite No. 3

2nd B♭ Trumpet

J. S. Bach
(1685–1750)
Trans. by A. Frackenpohl

© 2003 Canadian Brass Publications LTD
International Copyright Secured

CANON

Johann Pachelbel
(1653-1706)
arranged by Walter Barnes

2nd B♭ CORNET/TRUMPET

2003, 1988, Canadian Brass Publications LTD
International Copyright Secured

FANFARE
from ORFEO

2nd B♭ Trumpet

Claudio Monteverdi
(1567-1643)
adapted and arranged by Stephen McNeff

© 2003 Canadian Brass Publications LTD
International Copyright Secured

TRUMPET TUNE AND AYRE

Henry Purcell
(1659-1695)
arranged by Walter Barnes

2nd B♭ CORNET/TRUMPET

2003, 1988, Canadian Brass Publications LTD
International Copyright Secured

TRUMPET VOLUNTARY

Stanley
(1713-1786)
arranged by Walter Barnes

2003, 1986, Canadian Brass Publications LTD
International Copyright Secured

Trumpet Voluntary *continued*

TRUMPET VOLUNTARY

Jeremiah Clarke
(1673-1707)
arranged by Walter Barnes

2nd B♭ CORNET/TRUMPET

2003, 1988, Canadian Brass Publications LTD
International Copyright Secured

BRIDAL CHORUS
from LOHENGRIN

2nd B♭ Trumpet

Richard Wagner
(1813-1883)
edited by Canadian Brass

© 2003 Canadian Brass Publications LTD
International Copyright Secured

WEDDING MARCH

2nd B♭ Trumpet

Felix Mendelssohn
(1809–1847)
Adapted by Ryan Anthony

© 2003 Canadian Brass Publications LTD
International Copyright Secured

RONDEAU
(Theme from *Masterpiece Theatre*)

2nd B♭ CORNET/TRUMPET

Jean-Joseph Mouret
(1682-1738)
arranged by Walter Barnes

2003, 1988, Canadian Brass Publications LTD
International Copyright Secured

ALBASON FANFARE

Gottfried Reiche (1667-1734)

Trumpet in B-Flat

Trumpet in B-Flat - Alternate Key

Piccolo Trumpet in A - Original Key

© 2003 Canadian Brass Publications LTD
International Copyright Secured